Lucid Dreaming

Guide To Exploring Nonphysical Reality And Spiritual Out-of-body Experiences In Higher Dimensions

(A Guide To Lucid Dreaming For Better Sleep And Enhanced Creativity)

Modesto Contreras

TABLE OF CONTENT

What Is Lucid Dreaming?.. 1
Does Lucid Dreaming Pose A Risk? 17
Dream Signs 22
What Hinders My Progress?.......................................27
Advantages To Lucid Dreaming 31
Practice Daytime Memorization And Observation Skills 36
Techniques To Determine Reality..............................51
Why Do Some People Succeed While Others Fail?.72
What To Do When You Dream Lucidly 76
How Lucid Dreaming Can Be Beneficial 85
Make A Habit Of Reality-Checking. 102
Dreamscape Exploration And Top Few   Activities 111
The Definition Of Lucid Dreaming 130

What Is Lucid Dreaming?

Lucid dreaming was practiced prior to being documented. Ancient tales from African tribes recount how royals were visited by their forefathers in their dreams. Symbols and signs were utilized by Egyptians to interpret their dreams.

The origin of the practice, which involved cultural merging between various groups such as Muslims, Bantu, Canaanites, Pygmies, Portuguese, and Romans along the Nile routes of Ancient Africa, remains unclear.

Lucid dreams were considered divine omens for future predictions in several African cities, including Egypt. Lucid dreaming was considered a gift of wisdom or creativity for selected individuals in some Central African capitals. Lucid dreams were used for healing in Tibet and India. Dreams and lucid dreams held equal importance in ancient Greece.

Scientific discoveries reveal that these historical beliefs are neither entirely correct nor incorrect. Your beliefs hold the truth. Your beliefs determine your power. Interpreting your dreams can empower them to impact your life.

It begins with having the right mindset. Without acknowledging the significance of dreams, you won't be able to recall them, irrespective of scientific or religious beliefs. If you don't believe that you can connect with your nightmares, you won't overcome them, develop, or become liberated.

Dreaming can change your life. If you have faith in your dreams as a tool for foresight, they'll serve that purpose. Your belief in their ability to aid you determines their impact on your success. You must believe wholeheartedly. You hold the key to unlocking the full potential of your dreams.

The Science

Scientists didn't acknowledge lucid dreaming, despite its widespread recognition and advantages, until 1978 (kzt5196, 2015).

Cecilia Green in her 1960s study on false awakenings offered the initial credible explanation. Keith Hearne noticed eye twitching of a sleeping volunteer in 1975, providing the first scientific proof of psychic phenomena.

Volunteers, while asleep, were conscious of their dreams and reacted to them as evidenced by false awakenings and eye twitches. No practitioner had ever seen, studied, or clarified this prefrontal cortex activity during sleep. The community was surprised and many studies aimed to explore lucid dreaming further.

People didn't reveal the actual evidence. Most studies proving lucid dreaming's existence used cats. Scientists analyzed the brains of cats in various sleep stages using EEGs, MRIs, and EOGs. The prefrontal cortex of the brain remained active during sleep, as indicated by these scans.

Your cat's joke about killing you might not be a joke, as they may be aware of their actions in their recurring lucid dreams. The human scans produced identical results few years later. People can gain dream control by becoming conscious during their dreams, like cats.

How It Works

To have a lucid dream, activate your prefrontal cortex by realizing that you are in a dream.

How can you achieve lucid dreaming when it only happens during the fourth stage of sleep, when the brain is less active?

You can use various methods to stimulate your prefrontal cortex. Say affirmations before bed to confirm participation in lucid dreaming. Do you recall Gabba, the brain's gatekeeper that functions like the social hostess? RAS releases Gabba. When you affirm your intentions, the RAS will reduce Gabba's impact on incoming information, allowing for clearer thinking.

Is it too good to be true?

Consider this: Have you attempted to awaken naturally rather than relying on an alarm? You can regulate your wake-up time daily by commanding your body and through the coordination of your body clock and RAS in the brain. Anxious people created the alarm. The efficacy of lucid dreaming affirmations is comparable.

Analyzing both realistic and non-realistic environments is another method. Analyze new animations and distinguish between the unrealistic and realistic elements. Does the movie depict a flying pig? Can it actually happen? Do rabbits have the ability to paint rooms in the color blue? Do blue rooms exist? Practicing differentiating dreams from reality helps you sense whether you are in a dream. If the room isn't blue, you may be awake; but if pigs aren't flying, you're not dreaming.

Distinguishing reality from a dream can be difficult, especially if immediate access to the logical reasoning center is unavailable. The more you practice, the easier and faster your prefrontal cortex will awaken.

To experience instant entertainment, listen to frequencies between 25 and 40 Hz, which keep the prefrontal cortex active during the second and third stages of sleep.

Additionally, you can purchase or create tools to detect your sleeping state. The Sound Oasis Mask displays images that gradually brighten or dim to suit your sleep routine. The mask darkens sunsets while you doze off. The mask displays a sunrise image as you awaken. You can set a small light flickering through the night. These dim flashes will not disturb your sleep, but you can recognize them in your dreaming state. Identifying them in your dream state also confirms your state of sleep.

This also applies to scheduling a light bulb or phone alarm at a specific time. Set an alarm or light for a few hours before your wake-up time for optimal results. Turn it off and go back to sleep. You might find the results intriguing.

Lucid Dream Categories

Wake Initiated

Two types of lucid dreams have been theorized by scientists. WILDs occur when one maintains conscious and reflective thoughts during the process of falling asleep.

To initiate wild dreams, one must keep their mind conscious while falling asleep. Clear thinking and sleep are incompatible. Have you attempted to reason logically while inebriated or fatigued? It's almost impossible. Occasionally, a critical task can trigger your adrenaline and enable you to concentrate on it.

Dreams that are WILD function similarly. Desire and practice are necessary. Someday, you will feel more empowered as you personally experience it with a strengthened mind.

LUCID dreaming involves intentionally experiencing conscious and focused dreams. Initiating a lucid dream right after falling asleep requires exceptional dream mastery.

If you intend to have authority over your life, this is a skill you would desire. Easy transition between wakefulness and lucid dreaming is highly advantageous. Imagine what else you can achieve with such mind control.

I'll narrate my initial WILD dream tale to you. Five years after the retreat, it was Sunday. I accompanied my mother to church to bring her joy, despite it not being a routine for me.

We had a big Sunday lunch after we went home. My mother has always cooked a large Sunday meal.

I ate a lot and then went to lie down with a full stomach.

Gazing up from the floor mattress at her dilapidated ceiling, memories of all the damaged roofs I had slept beneath flooded my mind.

I chose to enter a dream, fly to the roof and repair it. My goal remained my focus.

I quickly left my body. I felt like a tethered phantom hovering over my slumbering body. I flew straight up through the ceiling. I focused my intent, love, and care on my hands, gazing above our roof at fluffy white clouds.

I used my hands to expand the tiles and patch the gaps on the roof. An internal force seemed to be pushing outward. My innermost being was lifted by a rope to fix our damaged roof under the vast expanse of the sky.

The hole closed and I returned to my body.

I sensed change as I woke up.

A three-room house in a good vicinity was made available for purchase at an unexpectedly low cost the next week. I put down a small deposit and, by some stroke of magic, I got it.

In my dream, I summoned the bravery to take the next move. I had faith in my ability to repair things, and I succeeded. A wild dream has such power.

Dream Initiated

DILDs occur spontaneously. Control and focus don't manifest DILD dreams. Planned dreams are not coerced like WILD dreams. A DILD dream can be experienced without requiring a concentrated and powerful state of mind. You need to be receptive to the world, fresh encounters, and new prospects.

DILD dreams comprise approximately 80% of lucid dreams.

To identify a DILD dream, think about it. You're having a DILD dream if you need small cues to realize that you're dreaming.

With WILD dreams, you instantly know where you are headed. You become aware of your dream state only while dreaming in a DILD dream.

You become aware of the dream's surreal nature during the DILD. You focus on objects, situations, writings, and images. A dream is never stable. Everything is constantly changing. Center and focus on one thing to reach lucidity.

You become an observer, participant, and director of your dream upon realizing that you are dreaming. You're now a confident, deliberate actor with your own plan. You become strong, resolute, and courageous.

Here's a DILD dream example from my early stages of practicing lucid dreaming.

A few months had passed since the retreat. I felt a strong need to regain control and power after the tragic loss of a family member. I desired to observe them. I hoped to dream of them to bid farewell while being aware of the dream state.

I sat daily in a circle of stones I made to WILD dream and communicate with my loved one. I didn't work. My prayers, pleas, and efforts bore no fruit.

I gave up one day. I slept to rest, closing my eyes with regret.

That's when it occurred.

I lay on my mattress, unbeknownst to me. I intended to sleep, and if not, I planned to stand up, but my arms lacked the power to elevate me.

I attempted to kick, yell, or shift. The struggle caused me to fall off my mattress sideways onto the floor. The tumble startled me. I rose above the floor to escape its presence.

I realized I was in a dream.

I flew through a mirror while trying out my new ability in the living room.

I witnessed some dreadful reflections in the mirror, but finally reached a place adorned with golden chrysanthemums, beloved by my departed spouse.

I saw them walking through the field with a basket of flowers while flying above in the blue sky and white clouds. I didn't call out. I don't know why, but I thought they were busy. All I needed was to see them happy and okay. I refrained from disturbing their sleep and mine.

I visualized myself in my physical form and suddenly appeared.

I woke up abruptly, gasping - I had fallen off my mattress. That heightened the reality of the experience.

Lucid dreaming aided my emotional healing and provided inner tranquility. DILD and WILD dreams hold equal value and benefits. Lucid dreaming relies on them for conception, practice, and mind control.

Does Lucid Dreaming Pose A Risk?

Is lucid dreaming unsafe? Are there any risks?

Lucid dreaming poses no harm. What happens in a dream stays within the realm of dreams.

Dreams cannot impact your physical form. Your body cannot experience death. Subject of your dreams

Perish, not your corporeal form.

Dying in a dream is the best thing that can happen. Life-changing and extremely beneficial. You are lucky to achieve it.

Some special situations may pose risks despite possible exceptions.

At lower levels of lucidity, you may mistake reality for dreams and believe that you are asleep while being awake. If you encounter a bear or a hostile dog, do not engage in roughhousing for fun or attempt to jump out of a window. Mistaking dreams for reality in such situations would result in fatality.

If unsure whether dreaming, avoid dangerous or risky behavior. And, if you are going to fly, always take off from the ground.

Everything hinges on how clear you are. Low-level fear is the only effect of lucid dreams. When completely conscious, you lack fear or confusion.

Individuals with mental health issues should avoid attempting lucid dreaming. Always consult your physician or mental health professional at first instead. If you have schizophrenia and struggle with distinguishing imagination from reality, lucid dreaming can exacerbate the condition, so caution is advised.

Working on non-lucid dreams is safer for everyone, particularly with the help of a therapist.

Intention's Power.

Successful journeys result from clear intentions. Intentions initiate all universal events.

Clear dreams can be achieved with intent and drive. Your intention energizes you, guides you, and leads you to triumph.

Tibetans performed energy creating rituals for their intentions. Our modern society has many traditions, such as school start, graduation, wedding, and birthday ceremonies, serving the same purpose.

You can generate positive energy by following an idol, reaching out to a teacher, or finding a supportive group. Value dreams and lucid dreaming by reading, watching videos, and discussing with friends.

Interest directs your attention. If you plan to adopt a dog, you'll notice more dogs around since they're what you focus on. Having an interest in lucid dreaming enables the creation of lucid dreams.

Be dedicated, persistent, and enjoy the process to achieve lucidity.

Let's form powerful intentions now.

Dream Signs

Four dream signs can help you achieve lucidity. Learn to identify dream signs and use them to induce lucidity in dreams. Dr. LaBerge devised a dream sign inventory for us to employ in accomplishing our lucid dreaming aim. Lucid dreamers recognize dreaming by using dream signs. These signs aid in achieving lucidity. They aid your rational brain in recognizing that a dream is happening.

What are dream signs? They could be diverse items such as a deceased relative, talking animals or fruit, an unusual door shape or a misshaped door handle. Recognize specific dream signs among millions that belong to you.

Dream signs are often personally significant and serve as cues that indicate you are dreaming. An item will be displaced from its usual location. Maybe the window's not there or the door's overhead. You will recognize it as peculiar.

Inner awareness comes first. You will notice an abnormality in the dream's thoughts, emotions, perception, or sensation. Example: imagining and then achieving levitation.

Action is the following dream sign. Some physical activities are incorrect. You or things in your dream, even objects, can fit the description. A scenario where people move backward and a dog flies on its leash while being walked is an example of this. Unusually action-packed.

The form is the third dream sign. It's typically related to one's appearance. Their body may have an odd shape or height, with extremely long arms that trail behind them during movement. Form often features shrunken heads.

The final dream sign is related to the context. It relates to your dreaming circumstance. A dream sign is something impossible or contrary to your real life. Anything conflicting with your waking life. Maybe you're trying scotch for the first time or dreaming of being a different gender. Once you're familiar with the sign, the dream context is clear.

We've discussed waking activities for lucidity and two can aid in identifying dream signs. The steps are concise and will assist you in recognizing your dream signs.

Let's start with a reality check. Be vigilant to detect anomalies while you're awake each day. Practice the reality check while watching sci-fi or supernatural TV shows from your couch. They will have various things out of place. Question their nature and all of them. A quick technique for dream enhancement.

Listing dream signs is the second technique. Your dream journal will serve as your catalogue. Identify dream signs and organize them into subgroups based on Dr. LaBerge's steps. The four are:

inner awareness, context, form, and action. Note down multiple dreams using this method and identify recurring symbols and the predominant dream category. This will aid you in recognizing your dream signs in lucid dreams. Find differences in your daily life to notice them more easily in your dreams, regardless of your most frequent dream signs.

What Hinders My Progress?

To teach people to bring out their inner strength, remove what currently exists. You must overcome the obstacle that repeatedly troubles you in life and appears in your dreams in order to achieve what comes effortlessly for you. In your case, a dark shadow of a person may be chasing you, similar to Tina's experience with her mother.

Focus on changing yourself first, for the time being. You were mentioned as a hindrance, and we'll tackle that issue first. To achieve your success, we need to defeat the dragon barring the castle to your prosperity. Killing your inner resentments, symbolized by slaying a dragon.

Your innate powers to activate your lucidity consciousness will be cancelled out by anger, hate, strife, and indifference. You need to heal some areas in your consciousness to achieve your dreams and desires, despite feeling calm.

How does feeling calm manifest during a traffic jam for someone who does not hold animosity? When someone confronts you with malicious intentions? By adapting what I teach, you'll repel negative people and feelings.

To defeat your dragon, we need to address the amygdalae, the core of the human brain. The amygdalae are the inner child's mental alert system, found in both left and right hemispheres. It guides us with past experiences to identify if someone we meet is a friend or foe, loving or hating.

Sadly, the amygdala can be misconstrued as others' intentions. They are confused because strangers have their own independent amygdalae for analysis. When facing any situation, there exist two distinct realities.

Meeting someone doesn't imply you have really met them, Adults' amygdala functions based on their innate sense of morality developed during infancy. Numerous homes worldwide have diverse opinions of what is right or wrong.

If you rely on your amygdala, then everyone you meet in life is partially incorrect. You consider these people especially incorrect if they contradict your upbringing. I'll show you how the amygdalae can make us seem like monsters to those we want to be seen as angels in the following section.

Advantages To Lucid Dreaming

Having lucid dreams has several benefits. You can enjoy controlling your actions and experience situations that were once only in your dreams.

Lucid dreaming's benefits have been identified by Stephen LaBerge too. These benefits are health and inner growth, creative problem solving and decision making, and wish fulfillment and recreation.

Health and inner growth

LaBerge calls lucid dreams 'healing dreams'. He thinks lucid dreaming can enhance both physical and personal development.

LaBerge says healthy living is not just maintaining the status quo. Lucid dreaming triggers imagination, similar to daydreaming and mental imagery. Lucid dreaming has been proven to bring about psychotherapeutic effects and positive changes to our health by mobilizing our latent inner powers, as stated by doctors David Bresler and Dennis Jeffe.

If our skills become inadequate, we instinctively search for new adaptations. Learning leads to personal growth and development, resulting in inner growth.

Problem solving, practice, and decision making

Lucid dreaming boosts creativity too. According to LaBerge, lucid dreaming boosts our creativity and innovation. During dreams, we can perform creative and flexible actions that are impossible while conscious in reality.

Lucid dreaming can improve creativity by encouraging us to engage in uncommon actions. Writing a book involves extracting an author's creativity and influences through scenario planning. Lucid dreaming stimulates creativity by generating novel thoughts and ideas.

Rehearsing something you fear in your dreams can benefit your performance, according to some. In dreams, you may freely pursue your desires without repercussions in reality. To prepare for an unknown speech day, practicing your speech in your dream can be helpful. Like this, you can witness the real occurrence. It's only in your dream, that's all. Practice there as if it's the real speech, and note down potential improvements for the actual delivery. Prepare for speech mistakes. Just rehearse in your dreams to avoid mistakes in real life.

Lucid dreaming aids in decision making. Sometimes, we struggle to make a decision due to our failure in considering multiple viewpoints. When we dream, we can test the potential outcomes of our choices and use them in reality.

Wish fulfillment and recreation

In our dreams, there are limitless possibilities. We cannot do something in our dreams due to the state of being asleep, unconscious, and unaware. Our dreams are decided by our pre-sleep brain and state of mind. When we have control in lucid dreaming, we can fully experience our dreams. Imagine the freedom and satisfaction of being able to do whatever you want in your dreams, regardless of how frequently you experience lucid dreams. The possibilities are endless!

You may desire to fly, but it's impossible to do so in reality. When you can lucid dream, you can fulfill any desire since dreams allow you to do anything.

Practice Daytime Memorization And Observation Skills

Practice being present is what you need to do next.

Take 5 minutes of silence during your spare time in the day and gaze at your hands. Repeat to yourself confidently, 'I will see my hands and realize I'm dreaming'.

Maintain focus and associate your hands with dreaming. Don't parrot it thoughtlessly. Stay focused and have belief in your words.

Train yourself to link the dream symbol (your hands) with lucidity and recognizing the dream state.

How to train yourself for this?

Ponder upon Pavlov's dogs? Ivan Pavlov demonstrated the possibility of learning through association via Classical conditioning.

Pavlov conditioned dogs to salivate at the sound of a bell paired with the presentation of food.

The dogs associated the sound of the bell with food and salivated in response. The bell elicited the dogs' salivation response.

The dogs linked the bell with the food through learning.

Your hands can serve as a LUCID trigger, just like the bell triggered the dogs. Associate your hands with being in a dream.

Practice increases awareness of current state of consciousness when looking at hands.

Third Essential Technique: Perform 3 Daily Reality Checks Endless Reality Verification

Reality checks confirm whether we are dreaming or awake. You can't push your index finger through the palm of your hand when you're awake, but it's possible in a dream. You cannot make your brown poodle levitate when you're conscious, but it's achievable in your dreams. Repetitively attempting to push your index finger through your palm or fly may result in attempting it during a dream. Perhaps you'll observe the unusual act of passing your finger through your palm or floating, and subsequently achieve lucidity. Regularly performing reality checks during the day can help you remember to do them in your dreams, leading to lucid dreaming. Examples of reality checks:

Select the habits that are easy to make permanent. Do your affirmations and repeat thrice daily.

Simple Reality Checks: finger through palm, fly attempt, repeated time/text check, hand clap attempt.

Try pushing your index finger through your hand when you encounter repeated numbers or letters like 1111, 12:12, AAA, EEE. Patterns like these are often located on license plates, clocks, phone numbers, and building addresses. In a dream, trying to push your finger through your hand can make you conscious of the fact that you are dreaming, letting you gain lucidity. Double numbers and letters are abundant, so utilizing this technique helps to cultivate the habit of performing reality checks frequently. Reality checks occur spontaneously, not requiring your intentional effort.

Check if the text/clock appears the same after briefly looking away. Clocks in dreams frequently freeze or alter time. Text is either blurry, unstable, or difficult to read.

Place sticky notes in common areas to remind you to perform reality checks. Perform reality checks whenever you come across these notes, such as pushing your finger through your palm, trying to fly, checking the time, and questioning if you're dreaming or awake.

Attempt to push your hand through the table surface every time you sit down. Your hand passing through in a dream can be a cue for lucidity.

Perform a reality check upon passing through each doorway. Often, the scenery behind the door changes or disappears when you look back at the entrance. You should become lucid upon noticing this.

Perform a reality check whenever you encounter a déjà vu or unusual situation in real life. If someone comes to mind and contacts you right away, perform a reality check. Dreams entail bizarre encounters. Reality checking in waking life can boost your chance of having a lucid dream.

Do your reality checks immediately after reciting your affirmations.

Eternal Reality Check

Using this technique will greatly improve your chances of lucid dreaming. Although doing reality checks 3 times a day is helpful, you must train yourself to check your reality constantly.

Perform a reality check on the written text/number pattern.

Text and numbers are ubiquitous in waking hours. Whenever you perceive any symbol. Briefly divert your gaze from the text and then return to it. Dreams often shift or blur. Initially, consistently reviewing written text for modifications can be exhausting. You're all set once it becomes a habit. Double/triple numbers or letters are commonly found, so keep an eye out for them.

Carry a dream item always for eternal reality checks. This is like the totems in Inception, such as the spinning top. This could take the form of a watch, necklace, bracelet, or miniature figure. Remember a detail about it. Assuming you consistently wear your watch on your left wrist. No watch on wrist could indicate you are in a dream. A change in the color of your bracelet from gold to silver could indicate that you are dreaming. Memorize the item's color, position, and weight. Regularly monitoring your desired object's color, placement, and weight can aid in attaining numerous lucid dreams. Carry your dream item in your pocket for wisdom. Putting your hands in your pockets is a reality check for lucid dreaming.

I now recall my dreams.

Make these seven words your mantra. Recite them to yourself at this moment. Intend to remember your dreams and keep it in mind. You have never been asked to recall your dreams. You haven't remembered them for that reason. I'm asking you. Most importantly, you're currently directing yourself. Prepare for your first dream-filled night by committing to remembering your dreams from now on. Place a notebook and pen beneath your pillow. It is crucial. When you wake up, visualize reviewing your dreams with eyes closed. You reach for your Dream Journal under your pillow right after opening your eyes. Record all dream events. Did you witness any unusual sightings, such as flying pigs or talking animals? How was the weather? What did you have on your feet? If there was no appearance, let it be. It's all OK.

People dream, but not all of them document it. Jotting down upon waking is crucial. Writing with a pen or typing affects the brain. You've boosted your cognitive awareness as the brain observes. Ask yourself as you contemplate your dream. Any noteworthy details indicating it was a dream in hindsight? I experienced a couple of lucid dreams a few weeks ago. The individuals in every dream donned aged golf footwear. In retrospect, it was evident. In the dream, I missed the chance to realize my lucidity and enjoy myself. Later, upon awakening, I discovered nine pairs of my old golf shoes in the house entrance closet. I disposed of three sets, donated three to Goodwill, and retained the remaining three. I was pleased with it. I'll soon golf again and release a Zen Golf Ebook. Guess what? I no longer dream about golf shoes. I'm using different signs now.

Recent brain research has monitored REM brain scans during lucid dreams. An average 8 hour night consists of 3-5 REM cycles. REM sleep increases as the night advances.

Communication with lucid dreamers during REM phase is achieved using signaling techniques. Whirling and rubbing hands can extend lucid dreaming. We joyfully rub our hands while washing them, just as we do in daily routine. Whirling is cleaning the backs of your hand with soap. Stop reading. Rub and whirl your hands for a scenery change, right away!

Choose whirling for changing venues. Rubbing is ideal for preserving the background. Upon awakening, I focus on keeping my eyes shut as the initial step. I seek dream sensory input and aim to re-enter. I gleefully rub my hands as pictures and the movie play. I frequently return to lucid dreaming. It's too tasty to give up.

The frontal lobes of the brain light up when dream subjects practice lucid dreaming, according to dream research. This occurs solely when the individual achieves lucidity and engages with the dream. The frontal lobes handle 'self' information. In lucid dreams, individuals explore details about themselves. Without clarity in the subject, the self remains uninvolved. Lucidly reflecting during dreams expands self-awareness and consciousness.

Exercise 1

1. Picture yourself all set for bed and ready to sleep. Perhaps you've organized a pile of documents. The family pictures

and other mementos are in sight. Under your pillow is your Dream Journal. You recline and contemplate. I have a relaxation room, which is nice. This place makes me feel cozy. This space belongs to my creativity. I recall my dreams now.

2. Breathe

3. You enter the pleasurable hypnagogic state. (Read slowly). Relax into your body and clear your mind of thoughts and personal narratives. You experience a feeling of floating and detachment. You become alert yet peaceful, as all your senses attune to tranquil energy. The essence of existence. I exist as I am.

4. You self-suggest. The ego takes the night off. Perhaps I'll abandon a greater portion of it. You are in the hypnagogic state, which is the onset of sleep. It's

lovely. You want to proceed with it. I recite 'I recall my dreams' in a hushed tone. My dreams will include awareness of my feet. Goodnight!"

Time passes

5. Upon hearing a bird's song upon waking, you realize that you shift dimensions. Pause to savor this moment. You're showing signs of waking, but you're not moving. You review dream images of yourself while figuratively frozen in the moment. Identify the dream signs. When could you have realized you were dreaming? Gratitude and motivation compel you to grab your Dream Journal and jot down this data. You wake up and grab your diary.

6. You dutifully jot down the information in your Journal.

7. You start rebuilding the dream using the previous dream's data. Perhaps you wish to alter the locations or inquire within the dream. The process always responds with love. You eagerly anticipate recalling the next dream, as gratitude overwhelms you. Do you have any questions about the choices in your life? Turn it into a visionary strategy. Inquire in a peaceful and reflective environment. I'll answer the question if you ask me directly. Just ask, that's all you need to do. Trust and believe. Your Soul will reveal answers in dreams and when awake.

Techniques To Determine Reality

Are Dreaming

Everyone experiences natural dreaming during sleep. It's easy to overlook dreams and not document them. Regular checks increase your awareness of your dreams. Reality checks can indicate if you are dreaming.

Self-Examination Check

Check your hands, arms, legs, and clothing. This aids in realizing when you're in a dream state. In dreams, you may wear clothes that are not in your actual wardrobe. Viewing the dream body's reflection reinforces lucidity.

Mirror Check

Find a mirror close by and examine yourself closely. Ask if you are awake or dreaming as you gaze at yourself. Often, you may perceive an unfamiliar image of yourself which could be shocking, such as an older, younger, unattractive or attractive form of you. Your altered reflection in a dream state indicates its unreality.

Gravity Check

Throwing up an object that should obey gravity is a useful reality check to perform while dreaming. If the object defies gravity and remains in the air, it indicates that you are dreaming.

Interrogating Your Dream Characters

You can ask your dream characters for a reality check. Some people who appear in your dream may not look as healthy as everyday people should. Noticing unusual traits of your dream characters makes recognizing a dream simpler.

The Penetration Check

The goal of a penetration test is to attempt to penetrate solid surfaces like walls, glass, metals, etc. with your fingers or palms. Your fingers can pass through surfaces effortlessly in a dream, impossible to replicate in a waking state.

Light Switch Check

Flipping a switch on a light bulb in your dreams indicates lucid dreaming. Malfunctioning switches are likely during dreams. Observe how the bulbs react to on/off instructions. You're dreaming if they don't match.

Performing these reality checks will determine if you experience lucid dreams. You can determine the required effort for reaching the next level of lucid dreaming at your own will. Let's explore methods to enhance your lucid dreaming and increase its frequency after learning reality checks for recognizing when you are dreaming.

Ways to Excel at Lucid Dreaming with Fundamental Techniques.

Trigger it frequently

To master lucid dreaming as a beginner, take specific steps. Effective lucid dreaming has no fixed formula, yet reliable tips exist to optimize your lucid dream experiences.

Here are efficient steps for practicing lucid dreaming:

Start with a journal to record your dreams.

To practice lucid dreaming, begin by keeping a dream journal. Keeping a dream journal improves memory and enhances dream awareness. Use the first few minutes of your morning to reflect on your subconscious thoughts instead of browsing your phone and social media. At first, recalling your dreams might not be innate. With dedication and time, remembering where you slept, with whom, and your role will get simpler.

Recording dreams in a journal aids in recognizing dream elements, helping to identify when in a dream. To maintain a dream journal, enhance your capacity to recall dreams.

Perfect the Skill of Recollecting Dreams

Remembering your dreams facilitates frequent lucid dreams. If you are not one of those lucky few who can easily remember their dreams, below are some tested techniques that can help you improve your dream recall abilities:

Master the skill of staying still upon waking up.

Delay opening your eyes upon waking. Stay completely still. Remain still for a few minutes before getting out of bed by keeping your eyes closed.

✓ Wake Slowly

Don't wake up abruptly and start thinking about your daily tasks. Gradually awaken and attempt to remember dream events. Thinking too much about the future can make it difficult to remember your dreams. Direct your thoughts towards your dream activities.

Keep the Dream Subject in Mind

Remembering the general theme of your dream - journey, meeting, date, adventure - can help you recollect further details such as location, people involved, time and purpose.

Complete Dream Checklist

Your dream list should feature people, places, and things that were on your mind the previous day, such as friends, food, movies, music, family, business, etc. The checklist can aid in recalling dream fragments related to checked items.

Try Different Sleeping Positions.

You can remember your dreams better if you maintain the same sleeping posture as you did during the dream. Experiment with different sleep positions to improve memory retention, starting with your initial position. If you woke up on your right, recall before switching to left, back, then front.

Bring your dream journal.

You can recall your dreams after being reminded by certain people, places, or events. It can occur any time of the day.

Keep your dream journal nearby to record memories upon recall. Writing more = Remembering more details about the dream.

Enhance Mindfulness and Awareness with Mindful Practice.

Meditation

Learning to induce lucid dreams is not the same as being able to maintain a desired duration within the lucid dream state. Mindful meditation can help prolong lucid dreams and enhance their benefits. Mindful meditation soothes and centers the mind. Mindful meditation helps you stay in your lucid dream.

When external factors like noise, sunlight, etc. can cause sudden wakefulness.

Mindful Meditation Practice Steps:

Mindful meditation is easy to practice. Follow these steps for better mindfulness and longer lucid dreams:

1. Meditate early in the morning for optimum results. Waking up earlier allows more time for mindful meditation. Meditation requires peaceful and private morning hours.

2. Choose a good location for meditation: The place you meditate in can affect your practice's success. Discover a tranquil location, free from interruptions, to practice meditation in your residence, workplace, or educational institution.

3. Prioritize your breaths: In meditation, it's crucial to prioritize and focus solely on your breaths, especially if you're a beginner. Concentrating on your breath enhances your ability to focus on the present and concentrate on a singular task. Concentrating on your breath aids

in relaxation and prevents the domination of thoughts about past mistakes or future uncertainties.

Lucid Dream Timing

Wake up at night and tell yourself you will lucid dream in the next 20 minutes to increase chances of lucid dreaming, suggests Dr Laberge from Stanford. This technique aims to make your dreams feel as vivid as reality. Upon achieving this, easily transition to a lucid dreaming state.

Frequent practice can aid in awakening and sleeping prior to dawn. Eliminating the boundary between your dreaming and waking states enables you to be conscious of your dreams and manage them efficiently.

Let's explore effective techniques for successful lucid dreaming.

3rd Technique: LaBerge's MILD

MILD, an acronym for Mnemonic Induction of Lucid Dreams, is a lucid dreaming technique created by Dr. Stephen LaBerge. He made this technique for beginners of lucid dreaming to boost their self-awareness and enhance their lucid dreaming experiences. How to practice this technique? Discovering the method:

Begin with Remembering Dreams and Verifying Reality.

Knowing Reality Checking makes you well-suited for practicing the MILD technique. If unfamiliar with reality checking, refer to previous section, recall dreams through journaling, and practice reality checking before proceeding.

Lucid Affirmations

At bedtime, acknowledge to yourself that you are conscious of your dreams and recognize that you are in a dream state.

This helps your subconscious acknowledge your awareness of dreams. Practice regularly and gain control over your mind to become conscious of your dreams. Below are effective suggestions to affirm your mind:

I will be conscious of my dreams.

I will become conscious during my next dream.

My next scene will be a dream.

Tonight, I will attempt lucid dreaming.

This moment is a dream.

Speak these affirmations with profound belief and feeling. Stronger emotions in your words build greater trust, and when faith powers your affirmations, your mind accepts them.

Repeat the chants before bedtime and concentrate on them. Repeat them until you feel yourself falling asleep.

Practice Visualization

When fully relaxed and drowsy, begin visualizing your dreams. Remember your last dream and imagine returning to it. Immerse yourself in vivid mental imagery, experiencing each moment as if it were happening again. Pay close attention to every small detail.

Focus on dream details and seek a sign of lucidity. A dream sign is often an uncommon character, item, or place that adds a surreal quality to your dream. Encountering a wizard or a unicorn are types of dream signs.

When you notice the sign, affirm 'I am dreaming.' Yet, persist in your dreaming. Pursue your dream and maintain your imaginative spirit. Before sleeping, remember to think about dreaming.

With consistent practice, you can gradually attain lucidity during dreams and dream consciously with ease.

Improve MILD Lucid Dreaming with this tip.

To enhance MILD lucid dreaming, awaken during sleep, attain full alertness, and return to sleeping. Interruptions during sleep ease lucid dreaming practice in MILD technique, as LaBerge discovered. Vomiting, meditating, and being intimate enhances lucid dreaming by increasing your consciousness and attentiveness towards yourself and surroundings, leading to better dream experiences. Make sure you sleep again after awakening.

Stay consciously awake for 15 to 20 minutes after using the bathroom and focus on the significance of lucid dreaming. Practice affirmations, visualize, and go back to sleep. You can set mid-sleep alarms. Use this tip to enhance your MILD practice.

If waking up becomes challenging and causes insomnia, pause the practice of this technique for at least a month.

4th Technique: Intentional Dreaming

Dreaming with intention is a highly effective method to practice lucid dreaming. It is simple, yet highly effective. It consists of setting the intention to lucid dream and using ideas and affirmations to facilitate the achievement of the state.

Let's examine this lucid dreaming method further.

Guide to Intentional Dreaming

Intent drives action. If you aim to be kind to others, you'll try to treat them with compassion and kindness. If you're determined to lose weight, you'll put in the effort to make it happen. If you aim to be consciously aware of your dreams, you will practice lucid dreaming. Intentional dreaming hinges on this. It utilizes your intent for clear and conscious dreaming.

Follow the steps below to practice intentional dreaming.

Intend your goal.

Intend to practice lucid dreaming to make your mind comprehend and embrace your goal. Intent is the commitment to perform a future act that exists in the mind. Forethought and planning make it up.

Intend to be aware in a chosen dream scenario while awake. This recurring activity will act as a dream sign to trigger your lucidity. If you dream of a lake frequently, aim to be conscious of your dream as soon as you encounter a lake in it.

Visualize the event multiple times a day to set your intention. Say to yourself that you're dreaming when your visualization is clear. You can achieve lucid dreaming with practice over time.

Every night tip: Do it.

Set your intention before sleeping to dream consciously. Specify your goals to set your intention. Is lucid dreaming a one-time experience or a lifelong desire for you?

Think about the question and give a good answer to create a clear goal for lucid dreaming.

I want to learn lucid dreaming and will work towards achieving it.

Speak clearly and naturally in your native tongue, and use a conversational tone.

Chant the affirmation loudly as per your situation, after setting your intention. Sleep in a different room or chant your intention in front of a mirror if you share a bedroom. As soon as you start feeling sleepy, you may return to your room. Practice talking to yourself before bedtime in a comfortable place like the shower.

Speak to yourself casually and as if you were talking to a close friend. As you gain comfort in yourself, your mind readily embraces it.

Tip: Talk to yourself in your first language regularly, as your mind readily understands and embraces the language you frequently use.

Advice: Maintain consistency.

Practice this every night consistently to engrain your intention in your mind. Make your mind adhere to your daily instructions. You will eventually find it effortless to enter a lucid dream state.

Tip: Thank yourself with gratitude.

Upon waking up, remember your dreams, write them down, and appreciate yourself for recollecting them. Thank you for recalling the dream so vividly and practicing lucid dreaming.

Thank yourself even for faint dreams or lack of lucidity. This practice affirms your mind's efforts and motivates it to follow your guidance more closely.

Express gratitude to yourself every morning for improved lucid dreaming.

Why Do Some People Succeed While Others Fail?

Some excel in their work, while others don't. Success does not require innate talent or uniqueness; anyone can achieve it.

Successful people share common traits, according to research. Can you identify it?

Imagine someone who is successful. Think of someone successful, such as a film star, athlete, Shakespeare, or Mozart. What makes them succeed?

It's persistence. Don't give up to be successful.

Tenacity is a common trait of success across various fields. They persevere through anything.

Successful lucid dreamers exhibit greater persistence. Your lucidity depends on your persistence. Your motivation and willpower determine it. Your desire is the key factor.

Only commitment to becoming lucid matters along with using the correct methods. With devotion, the universe yields to you.

Typical learning curves start out steep and become gentler over time, according to psychologists. Acquiring new abilities requires constant repetition and is never effortless.

Mastering lucid dreaming requires balancing focus and determination with calmness and nonchalance, which can be challenging. If your mind is too eager, it can be difficult to fall asleep, and your excitement may awaken you when you realize you are lucid.

You'll achieve balance with practice.

Dream Interpretation

Dream interpretation is common in numerous dream traditions. We advise against it as it disrupts healing and impedes significant transformation.

Dream analysts interpret dreams, while Dream Yoga practitioners engage with the dream material itself during lucid dreaming.

Interpreting dreams depends on individual and personal factors such as history, life events, and subconscious imprints. There are no universal dream symbols.

Hasty and useless conclusions may result from intellectual dream interpretation. Allow your subconscious to decipher the message behind your dreams at a gradual pace instead. Reflect on dream characters and events to aid your subconscious. Could they have valuable teachings for you? Which memories do you associate with them?

What To Do When You Dream Lucidly

Dream commands:
I briefly mentioned dream commands in my previous entry. When you yell something aloud to your dream, that is a dream command. Your belief in your dream determines its obedience. Lucid dreamers often use this technique to become aware and accomplish difficult tasks. By using them as questions, you can learn something new about yourself. Be cautious with the information you share with the dream. Don't scare or trap your dream, as it will react accordingly. Sharing your dream can create an illusion of being trapped by it. Be cautious with your subconscious mind.
Mirrors:
Exercise caution and mentally prepare by dedicating a dream specifically for this. In dreams, the reflection in a mirror may not resemble your physical

appearance. I won't do it because of my low self-esteem and the resulting distorted image. Mirrors could reveal frightening reflections, so be cautious.

Practicing Skills:

If you've experienced it before in reality, practicing life skills in lucid dreams is an option. My source used lucid dreams to practice driving and passed the driver's test faster than without the dream practice. It may seem absurd, but it's effective.

Summoning/Manifestation:

I'm consolidating these two since they're practically identical. You can create things out of thin air by belief when fully lucid. That's manifestation. You can apply the same technique to bring people or objects from reality into your dream. To summon better, try visualizing a closed door, imagine the thing or person behind it, and then reopen the door. Appearances can be deceptive.

Flying:

Don't lie. Lucid dreamers have either tried or intend to try this. Believe you can fly and you will, just like with manifestation. There are several flight descriptions available. You're motionlessly airborne, similar to levitation, which is the flight commonly anticipated but not experienced yet, like my initial lucid dream. I've heard it can be like walking on an unseen staircase. Perhaps it's your technique. I cannot advise on take-off as my only lucid dream involved me already in the air. But once you're airborne, there should be no difficulty.

Teleportation:

That's a goal of mine. I desire to master flight, teleportation, and dream controls. To teleport, spin around or imagine spinning, then picture a location. When spinning, vision momentarily fades, making this technique effective. You will teleport then. Wait until your dream is stable before attempting this, as getting dizzy could disrupt it and teleportation requires a stabilized dream state.

Speak with dream personas:

You can converse with the dream characters anytime. A fascinating notion is to induce lucidity in a dream figure alongside yourself. Some dream characters gain the ability to act independently and have the same powers as the lucid dreamer, leading to intriguing interactions. It appeared eerie yet impressive.

Avoid These During Lucid Dreaming.

Here are a few things to avoid in lucid dreams to prevent potential fear, premature end, or later confusion:

Don't close your eyes. Not frequently or repeatedly in quick succession. You will be awakened by this.

Avoid dreaming about actual people or situations. That can eventually cause confusion between memories and dreams. It would be uncomfortable to mention a dream occurrence to someone who was not involved.

Avoid using imperative statements like "trap me" or "scare me" in dreams. I've reviewed this and it'll succeed.

Refrain from engaging in excessive excitement (e.g. sexual activity). It will also cause you to become alert.

Avoid premature utilization of your abilities. Typically, this causes the dream to end, either from personal vexation or incorrect execution of the technique. I acknowledge my guilt and suffered the consequences. Teleporting requires spinning, as mentioned below. If you fly prematurely, you'll tumble, panic, and awaken. At worst, manifestation will only bother and wake you up.

Limit lucid dreaming. It doesn't bother me as I have difficulty achieving clarity, but for those with greater ability, it may pose a challenge. You'll lose interest in either lucid dreaming or reality. This is frequently cautioned and therefore noteworthy.

Avoid harming yourself physically. Pain, even in dreams, can discourage lucid dreaming. Violence in dreams can rewire your brain for violence in real life. Lucid dreaming may provoke violence. It provides stress relief, but caution is advised.

Focus your mind away from your physical form. This can wake you up and is said to be linked with bedwetting, although the source is reliable.

Unrestricted Enjoyment and Excitement. Experience all your desired pleasures. Practicing dream control creates a colorful mental playground from your subconscious. Encounter anyone, soar amidst the cosmos, satisfy your deepest desires.

Unrestricted! Unpunished! Unrestrained!

E

Your brain can create detailed imagery, scents, sounds, and tastes that are truly astonishing. You may experience strong physical feelings, like the adrenaline rush of flying or the enjoyable sensations of sexual activity.

Treating Nightmares
Lucid dreaming treats nightmares. People often have trouble sleeping

because they fear experiencing nightmares. Lucid dreams aid in conquering fears by providing the individual with control over their dream and sleep.

The dreamer becomes empowered. Lucid dreaming eliminates nightmares. Let me explain.

Lucid dreamers can distinguish between dreams and reality. They can distinguish between their dream and reality. During these nightmares, they maintain lucidity and observe the events as if watching a scary movie, aware that it is not real. They can totally dominate the dream. They have complete authority to steer and navigate it in any direction they desire.

Take Creative Leaps

Normalcy is unusual in a lucid dream. You can challenge physics laws or invent new creatures. You can change time's flow or choose the next president by counting fishes caught using bare hands. Interesting, right? Everything is permissible.

Anything is possible as long as you can imagine it.

You'll be astounded by how amazingly imaginative and creative your brain may be during lucid dreams after this.

Keep in mind that when you lucid dream, logical barriers are broken down, creating the ideal setting for the best out-of-the-box ideas and stories. You can come up with fresh concepts for stories, business solutions, professional insights, and whole different approaches to solving issues. Research has shown that those who frequently have lucid dreams answer a considerably higher proportion of insight problems than those who do not.

How Lucid Dreaming Can Be Beneficial

Lucid dreaming has numerous benefits which makes it difficult to limit them. Reducing the benefits of lucid dreaming to a mere list would not do justice to its true value, which is a profound and enriching experience. Nevertheless, I'll illustrate and explain the significance of lucid dreaming and its worthiness of being learned.

Dreaming lucidly enhances consciousness. Lucidity means being more aware. You realize you're dreaming. Lucid dreaming is not just imaginations beyond reality. Numerous studies have reported additional benefits of lucid dreaming.

Knowing about the Self is necessary to understand the benefits. The self is a process, not a static entity. You are not only the present you, but also all your past selves. You exhibit different moods such as anger, happiness, sadness, hunger, etc. You are a group of identities coexisting in one household. Integration increases as harmony among them grows.

Consider your familiarity with your mind. Explore your subconscious mind (via dreams) to test and question this effectively. You remain yourself while dreaming, as your mind creates the dream materials. If you don't remember your dreams or experience lucid dreams, you may not be fully connected with that aspect of yourself.

When you dream, you can get to know your subconscious and explore the unknown. Your mind creates high-quality, imaginative dreams every night, full of information. They are far from being random.

Lucid dreaming allows you to make anything possible by interacting, manifesting, and altering whomever or whatever you desire. The greatest advantage appears to be the chance to become the ultimate version of oneself. Being able to CONTROL your dreams is invaluable!

Fringe Benefits

Lucid dreaming yields daily positive outcomes. You'll witness an incremental improvement in yourself through augmented curiosity, courage, and openness, along with diminished fear, worry, and closed-mindedness. Observing and participating consciously results in becoming familiar, connected, and understanding. It's uniting with the unacknowledged or ignored facets of your mind or self that you were aware of.

Lucid dreaming enhances life's purpose, meaning, and value. It's similar to improving your physical fitness and experiencing a positive change in your daily well-being. Or when starting a new relationship and feeling more energetic. You feel content with everything around you.

Numerous individuals practice lucid dreaming currently. Interest in lucid dreaming is increasing due to its benefits and supporting research, leading to a growing number of practitioners.

Lucid dreaming helps conquer fears and phobias.

Are you afraid of heights? Why not jump out of an airplane in your dreams if you fear heights? You are safe and can control your fall, slowing down time and landing gently. At 10,000 feet, lucid dreamers have reported improved confidence regarding heights while awake. Facing the worst-case scenario helps form positive neural patterns in your unconscious, aiding in long-term fear reduction.

Able to assist in solving important issues / making vital choices.

Many mathematicians and scientists consider this the best benefit of lucid dreaming. Visualizing a particular problem while dreaming was deemed a crucial advantage by them. That process creates fresh neural connections, enabling diverse approaches and notions to address essential issues or take critical decisions.

You can use lucid dreams to solve problems by experimenting with different solutions and observing their outcomes within the dream. Dream refinement can implant questions or problems in your subconscious. When you assign a task, your subconscious will work on finding a solution that will be communicated to you via dreams.

Enhance existing skills through practice. Can you agree that practicing real-life skills in dreams can improve them when awake? This is a remarkable and astonishing benefit of lucid dreaming. You can attend music lessons in reality and practice what you learned in your lucid dreams. This advanced learning could expedite your understanding of the instrument compared to conventional learning methods. You can improve as a musician while saving money and time. Using lucid dreams, you can improve your skills in various areas of life.

The mind is active during REM sleep. Consider it from an evolutionary perspective. Why does nature select us for dreaming simulated mental realities? Is it essential for the species as a whole? I believe so and here's my reasoning.

What is the function of the mind during dreams? I researched extensively for this book and believe Antii Revonsuo's Threat Simulation Theory of Dreams is an excellent way to define what dreams are.

Dreams are mental representations of different versions of reality. Dreams, though seemingly vague and sporadic, can reveal significant understanding about one's waking life when closely analyzed. By focusing on their dreams, humans can uncover authentic significance, intention, and worth.

REM Sleep helps in memory consolidation and prioritization by ranking memories based on their significance. Dreaming is a useful and flexible mental procedure.

How does lucid dreaming aid in strategy development? Your brain strategizes and organizes while dreaming. It could be more efficient and effective. You can awaken your conscious mind within the dream simulation by achieving clarity and recognizing that you are dreaming. You can intervene and intentionally make what you consider to be the most significant outcome.

Compare the lucid state to a video game. You are both the main character and the environment, challenges, obstacles, and bosses in the game. You lucid dream and play the game yourself with a vague recollection upon awakening.

What aspect do you wish to enhance? Your creative abilities? A sport? A relationship? Perhaps your relationship role? You're already dreaming of them. When lucid, summon it forth within the dream by requesting something to dream about, and use the opportunity to practice, rehearse and enhance your skills.

Stephen LaBerge includes a doctor's account of practicing surgery in his sleep in his book, Exploring The World of Lucid Dreaming. Due to this, he gained a reputation of excellence and could hone his techniques quicker than other surgeons. Improved physical skills transfer to muscle memory for real-life application with clear efficacy. Likewise, you can realistically rehearse mental and emotional responses while lucid to enhance skills like public speaking. Perfecting your skills is possible through dreaming about practice.

Overcome/stop nightmares

I think practicing lucid dreaming has a significant impact for this reason. You can conquer nightmares while you sleep. 50-85% of adults and higher in younger people experience occasional nightmares.

Many have repeated dreams and bad dreams that feature anxiety-inducing scenarios such as plummeting from a frightening precipice or being pursued by someone or something. Mastery of lucid dreaming allows intervention in nightmares. Furthermore, you can modify them for positive results.

You can win the battle and remove your nightmare as you have full control over the situation.

What are nightmares?

Bad dreams portray real-life problems and cause unease, known as nightmares. A nightmare could be your subconscious mind alerting you to a serious concern that needs urgent attention - it might be a fear or worry that you haven't yet resolved during your waking hours.

Nightmares can persist and cause distress, even though the subconscious may occasionally solve such issues independently.

Lucidity amidst a nightmare alters the experience, though it may remain initially scary. It's not happening. It's a dream, you know. It's a reality. It's your dream. You realize you can control how the interaction proceeds. This choice component reduces fear and intensity, if not eliminating them.

Engaging with terrifying entities

Scary characters like demons or monsters symbolize a real-life issue you're facing. It's just a copy.

Nightmare personalities are parts of yourself your mind creates, so being kinder to them means being kinder to a part of yourself that's struggling. If you become lucid, simply halt, pivot and confront them. Show them kindness, love, and acceptance. Inquire about their embodiment and how you may aid them.

You are shifting the focus from a scary situation to a positive and fruitful dialogue. You're not just changing your stance, but also transforming yourself. You transform from a victim to a capable obstacle remover in the dream. It's safe and feasible due to its existence in the dream simulation.

Learning to reframe lets you reconsider and reinterpret unpleasant experiences, not just in dreams or aspirations but also while awake.

Lucid dream sex

Lucid dreaming enhances sexual satisfaction and is a perk of this practice. What if you could have complete freedom in choosing anyone and any location without any restrictions or repercussions, fulfilling your desires as you please? Lucid dreaming allows you to realize your dreams in clear and sensory-rich detail by controlling them through your mind's simulation. In a dream, you can have sex with anyone and anytime you desire.

Sex and intimacy serve as strong lucid dream triggers, as you typically only expect to be with your partner in your waking life (if you have one). Kissing someone in your dream indicates that you are dreaming.

Not all idol meetings are purely academic or inspirational. Summon any partner for lucid dream sex and enjoy the release it provides.

People have innate strong sexual urges. We do not consciously select our sexual orientation, preferences, urges, or desires, just as we do not crave food, sleep, or social interaction. Our sexual instincts are inherent traits that we possess due to genetics and biology. Sexuality frequently appears in dreams for lucid practitioners.

Dream adventures are REAL at the level of the brain. Wet dreams are undeniably real, regardless of how much credit they are given.

Is having enjoyable dream sex in the privacy of your subconscious unwise, considering the significance of using time wisely in the lucid state? Isn't it wise to integrate without involving sexuality? Lucidity during dreams has a valid advantage.

Why deny or rationalize our urges instead of acknowledging them? We naturally have sexual fantasies; it is normal to enjoy them.

Lucid dreaming sex can help control urges and impulses, serving as a form of self-management. If we lack self-awareness and self-control, our instincts can take over and lead us to regrettable actions. Safely acquainting with it, integrating with it, and genuinely feeling comfortable with our sexuality is much preferable.

What if you have a partner?

Consider this point: Great intimate relationships involve more than just sex. What aspect of your sexual relations do you intend to improve, practice, and refine while sleeping? How can you better serve someone you love? Experiment with creative methods while lucid. You understand what I mean.

Dangers of having sex in a lucid dream

Many people are motivated to learn lucid dreaming because they can have sex with anyone. Yet, dangers such as addiction, escapism, immoral behavior, preference for dreams, among others, exist. If you plan on learning lucid dreaming, be careful of not enjoying it excessively. Further research and discussion on this topic is necessary. Maintain moderation in all things and use your time wisely.

Heal Emotionally Through Lucid Dreaming

Not everyone knows about the emotional healing potential of lucid dreams. Emotional healing is the ability to self-repair psychological wounds. You can heal fear, stress, doubt, and trauma through lucidity.

Individuals may have varying results. Some individuals may require additional processing time due to experiencing severe trauma, but it remains a possibility. Lucid dreaming can be considered as a tool for dealing with any ailment, be it chronic or minor.

You can heal through intention or dream doctor. The placebo effect proves the power of the mind.

Assume you feel frustrated about various work-related changes. You can express your anxieties to your co-workers and boss freely as you are in control of the dream. You may feel more empowered and find a solution applicable to your real-life situation.

Discovering your true self

The subconscious mind is an important and powerful part of the brain. The subconscious controls bodily functions like temperature and breathing by interpreting millions of brain signals per second. The subconscious mind controls your emotions and feelings beyond your complete control.

Communicate with your subconscious as a person through lucid dreaming. That's why lucid dreaming is an important practice. In lucid dreams, subconscious projections of non-self entities depict traits dissimilar to oneself. Lucid dreamers note a hidden awareness within dreams. This insightful self speaks candidly and alludes to both waking and dream elements.

Lucid dreaming is referred to as a separate consciousness by Robert Waggoner. I see it as my true self. Childhood-formed false beliefs obscure acquired knowledge. What questions would you ask if you had great clear insight?

Finding personal meaning in life is helpful.

Lucid dreaming may reveal the purpose of your life. Life's purpose begins with one's own interpretation, Lucid dreaming enables you to pursue your life's purpose with awareness. In lucid dreaming, you can view your future goal. Lucidity enables real-time examination of dreams, rather than waiting until awakening. You can interact and question your subconscious with this real-time analysis.

Utilize your lucid dreams to strengthen your waking beliefs - to understand the purpose. Why is my purpose? What purpose does my life serve? Who am I?

They exist for exploration through dreaming. Clever stuff.

Enrich your innovativeness
Unlimited dreams can materialize instantly.
You can easily manipulate and visualize ideas in your mind with effortless rearrangement, creation, and deletion.
Albert Einstein's theory of relativity was inspired by his imagination of riding on a light beam.
Yesterday's melody was composed by Paul McCartney in a dream.
Niels Bohr attributed his discovery of the atom's structure to an inspirational dream.
Lucid dreaming boosts creativity. You are very creative, even if you don't realize it. Trust your dreams to reveal the truth, not just my words.
Your mind creates vivid pictures and innovative concepts for two hours every night, despite your eyes being shut in dreams. Your mind is creating every dream detail. Imagination is the source of such unimaginable creativity.

In a lucid state, you can use your imagination without limits. Discover your exceptional creative capabilities and exceed your own expectations.

You can freely explore inventive ideas without waking life's boundaries or guidelines. It's your simulation, solely created by your mind; therefore, you make the laws. You can create anything in this setting, as you are its Creator. Produce imaginative works in various forms using detailed visualization and real-time creativity.

What if I lose my imaginative dreams?

Lucid dreams are typically recalled more vividly than non-lucid ones upon waking. To boost your creativity, experiencing the lucid state is essential.

Enjoying oneself and achieving the UNACHIEVABLE.

Lucid dreaming is immensely enjoyable. Do whatever you want without any fear of harm or mistakes. You may have unlikely experiences and wake up with incredible dream memories.

Your excessive stress can sometimes make you completely devoid of enjoyment. Happiness and relaxation are essential for a fulfilling life. Escape through lucid dreaming. Fun is fast and free. Furthermore, it won't detract from your critical conscious periods.

You can choose to road trip the US, sail a yacht, ski the Swiss Alps, or dance in a club in your dream.

The world of dreams is mysterious and full of peculiarities to explore. Enjoy and discover. Relax and compensate. It's worth enjoying your dreams to wake up feeling stress-free and happy.

Make A Habit Of Reality-Checking.

The fun begins now. Multiple reality checks are available. I'll share my favorite but use your own preference. Performing reality checks while awake trains your mind to do them automatically while dreaming. When you dream, the test fails. An Aware dream will be created spontaneously.

In dreams, we perceive everything as reality. If your shirt turned into Laffy Taffy, your perception of reality would be challenged. Our dreams reflect the beliefs we hold in waking life. The constraints we have in dreams are non-existent. We realize we are dreaming when the framework of our reality is shattered. That's what reality check habits are for.

The breathing check is my preferred reality check. Pinch your nose and attempt to inhale. If you aren't dreaming, you can't breathe through your nose; if you are dreaming, you'll be able to breathe normally.

Believe you might be dreaming, even if you're sure you're not, when developing a reality check habit. Pinch your nose closed and try breathing through it. Confirm your ability to breathe through your nose, not that you are not dreaming. When you dream, you feel as certain about being awake as you currently do. My initial reality checks involved using an hourly beeping Casio watch. I would perform a reality check when it beeped. I realized I was dreaming when my watch beeped on a hiking trail. Excited, I ran to the cliff edge. I hesitated to jump and check if I could fly due to fear. I double-checked my reality to avoid a news headline reading 'Man jumps off cliff on hiking trail'. I stood at the cliff's edge, about to leap, convinced it was a dream. I was mesmerized by the landscape's beauty as I looked out. The mountains' hue, the wind's touch, the chill on my face. I refrained from jumping off the cliff as I wasn't completely certain that it was a dream and I didn't want to take a chance. I had a vivid dream where I admired a breathtaking landscape and realized it was all created by my mind. Upon waking up, I felt amazed and filled with appreciation for nature, which stayed with me for days.

Try these reality check options.

Block your nostrils with your fingers and attempt to inhale. (my favorite)

Attempting to penetrate solid objects using your finger or hand.

Check the time on your watch twice, did it alter? While dreaming, time can jump from 3:45 to 8:58 in an instant.

Does your reflection match your face? Your face in dreams may alter or vary frequently.

Pinch yourself and check for pain. (a classic)

Summarize Creating Reality Check Habits

Select a reality check and perform it repeatedly during the day, preferably every one or two hours. You can do it whenever it comes to mind. Use a watch with hourly beep reminders to prompt reality checks.

Stay receptive to the idea of being in a dream during reality checks, regardless of your certainty of being awake.

Don't let early test failures disrupt your excitement or motivation for achieving your dreams. Simply embrace the process and stay focused, because there will be other chances in the future.

Aware Dreams

Lucid dreams are dreams in which you are aware of the fact that you are dreaming, but you might not have complete control over your actions or surroundings. In lucid dreams, there can be feelings of haziness and sudden awakening when attempting actions. The more you have aware dreams, the easier it becomes to achieve lucidity.

The difference between Lucid and Aware dreams is significant. An Aware dream cannot be confused with a Lucid dream. Lucid dreams are vivid while Aware dreams may lack impact. Lucid dreams can be accessed through conscious dreams, which may still lack excitement compared to typical dreams. Some who claim to have had Lucid dreams actually experienced only Aware dreams, as reported to me. A person told me about their lucid dream, which they didn't enjoy. I asked for more information and confirmed it was an Aware dream.

People who forcibly attempt lucid dreaming tend to have more conscious dreams, although almost everyone experiences them while trying to achieve lucidity. Conscious dreaming is an ideal platform to hone the mental skills required to attain dream control and achieve lucidity. Repeating statements to yourself can help trigger a lucid dream while being aware in a dream.

I have a specific Aware dream in mind. My reality check failed while standing on a New York balcony in an apartment complex. The spacious balcony overlooked trees and adjacent apartment balconies. I realized I was in a dream, but the colors and vibrancy faded away. I repeated the phrase 'I want clarity now!' multiple times until the dream became vivid and I became lucid. The leaves and stone became 100 times brighter, while the sounds of birds chirping and cars honking filled my ears. All was thriving!

Aware dreams can lead to discouragement and feelings of failure, so it's important to highlight them. After 3-4 weeks of attempting a Lucid dream, if all you had was a mediocre Aware dream, it's simple to quit. Aware dreams lead to Lucid dreams, so allow them to come naturally without any effort or forcing.

Aware Dreams Summarized

Lucid dreams are those in which you are aware that you are dreaming but lack control over the environment or experience fuzzy and dull surroundings.

Experiencing an Aware dream should not discourage you, as it is a natural progression towards Lucidity.

Shout repeated affirmations like 'clarity now' or 'vividness now' during lucid dreaming.

If you're having an Aware dream, avoid attempting a Lucid dream as it can disrupt the dream.

Dreamscape Exploration And Top Few Activities

Let's pause and appreciate the scenery after examining objects and dream characters. You can either envision the scenery your unconscious mind creates, or you can select one yourself. Their collision in your lucid dreaming creates a blend of their characteristics.

This chapter discusses your location and the top 10 activities in the dreamscape.

The topography

Your dream landscape can include a shopping mall, your high school, a farmer's field, or a mountaintop. It's your subconscious mind that determines the content of your dreams. Elements of all dreams can spontaneously appear during lucid dreaming. You can modify the details in lucid dreaming as per your liking.

Your mindset upon entering the lucid dream holds great significance. What is important to you right now? What are your current thoughts and life goals? What brings you joy? Do you feel optimistic?

Your mindset and how you handle it is vital for lucid dreaming and reaping its benefits. Your success in lucid dreaming depends on your state of mind, which is crucial whether your goal is psychological healing, ongoing peace, or improving your life status. And you're involved significantly in that.

Our moods are not solely determined by external factors, as we have the power to decide how we react to life's ups and downs. Either choose victimhood or rise above life's challenges and setbacks. You can use lucid dreaming to aid you. The dream itself is what matters, it will teach you. Your state of mind and lucid dreams can both aid you in overcoming challenging situations and finding a path forward. It's a powerful tool that can help you realize and achieve self-fulfillment.

Your playground in the world of lucid dreaming is determined by the lay of the land. You are the creator, manager, and casting director of the dream world.

Review physical elements in your dreamscape and identify their personal and global significance.

Mountains

Mountains have rich symbolic value in both conscious and unconscious realms. Martin Luther King Jr. used the story of Moses not being able to enter the Promised Land despite leading his people there as a biblical analogy. He spoke his final words in Memphis before being shot on the Loraine Hotel balcony by James Earl Ray, saying 'I may not get there with you.' And he did not. His work caused significant change. Dr. King's pioneering efforts have brought us closer to realizing freedom, despite the fact that the Promised Land remains elusive for some.

Mountain views are spectacular when incorporated into a dream world. They remind you to hold on to what matters to you. Are you trying to prove something to others by climbing a metaphorical Everest? You're not benefiting from the effort if that's true. It's sacrificing your confidence and vitality to please external opinions on your achievements.

Snowy peaks suggest forthcoming change and prosperity. Don't fear change, embrace it when ice and snow appear on your mountain landscape. Change is certain like the mountains.

When you encounter a wildflower-filled alpine meadow in the mountains, you feel a desire for liberation. You're holding onto comfort despite being at the brink of change in a job, relationship, or other life circumstance. Stop hesitating and level up towards the open spaces of the mountains in your dreams.

Hills

Unknown is symbolized by rolling hills. Unknown things in hidden valleys and gorges cause anxiety for dreamers because fear often stems from the unknown in reality and in dreams. We tend to avoid exploring dark spots like gullies.

Your interaction with the rolling hills matters. Do you wonder and imagine about the secrets in their gullies? Do you avoid crevices between hills, even if it means taking a longer route?

Most of us find the unknown frightening. We avoid uncertainty and ambiguity as we cannot control them. Prioritizing safety over exploration leads to considerable soul decay. Consider if hills in your dreams signal a need for spiritual growth and joyfully investigate.

A Garden

A garden can serve as a query, a response, or a representation. Your dream's garden is urging you to attend neglected aspects of yourself. Watering that part of yourself can make it appear, like a beautiful garden.

The garden answers our profound, unresolved queries. Typical queries focus on philosophical matters related to human nature, such as sexual orientation, career path based on abilities, and the objective of developing one's talents. The garden may also involve marriage and children. The garden may provide a definite answer if unsure. Your answer could be a flower, plant, or bird. A dream character may ask you another question. The garden prompts the necessary queries for you to become true to yourself.

The garden conveys a semiotic message. A flourishing garden represents both abundance and transience. In lucid dreams, the message is personalized and can be controlled by the dreamer, but it universally symbolizes growth, new beginnings, and the cyclical nature of life.

A withering garden can represent death and decay, or like a flourishing garden, the endless cycle of life. The garden's condition, whether dying or dead, could indicate a potential change, positive or negative.

Let's move on to your responsibility as the architect of your dream world after exploring some classical landscape elements that appear in our dreams, whether lucid or not.

Spawning the Dreamscape

When producing dream elements, ensure that you concentrate enough without compromising the quality or stability of your lucid dream. This was emphasized in the chapters on dream objects and dream characters.

Remember to take on only what you can handle to stay stable. Stick to what you can visualize readily to enhance your manifestation skills, as stated in the preceding chapters.

We use our existing knowledge as a foundation. All our skills are based on our existing knowledge of a subject. Lucid dreaming folllows the same pattern. Familiarity with your goal is key to effectively creating and controlling its features.

You can begin dreamscapes by altering elements like including trees, plants, and animals. You can replace rolling hills with a meandering river in a valley if you prefer familiar terrain. Alternatively, you may choose to fly to nearby mountains from an alpine meadow. Focus on visualizing an element that is easy for you to create in your dream.

Your dreamscape doesn't have to follow real-world logic, as shown by a real-world example. You may choose to have the Roman Coliseum in your alpine meadow. It's your dream. Using your existing abilities, construct it based on your own vision.

Your dreamscape could be a garden in your world, perhaps your own. Your self-planted and care-tended garden is the perfect dreamscape since you own and cultivate it. You can control the garden in your dreams as you know it so well. A familiar garden can serve as a great backdrop for creating objects and characters. Familiarity with the garden provides a clear outline for your lucid dreaming pursuits.

Memorable experiences and places can serve as great inspiration for manifesting your dream destinations. Your extensive knowledge of a subject can be a powerful aid for lucid dreaming. It establishes your world in the realm of dreams and provides a basis for enhancing your creativity in that realm.

Let's discuss the Top 10 Dream Activities. These are just initial ideas, as I expect you to come up with more of your own. Let's explore captivating methods to encounter the dream world!

Converse with Heroes, Villains, and Deceased Kin

Although lucid dreaming is not a séance, we all desire to meet our beloved heroes, don't we? Do you want to punish evil individuals from history and present by causing explosions or dropping heavy objects on them? If you want to vent, the lucid dream realm is a safe space since it's your dream.

Your grandma may have died without giving you her popular divinity fudge recipe. Could a dream visit spark some memories that aid a skilled dreamer, even if they don't entirely recall the recipe? Otherwise, you would be conversing with your grandmother, right?

Before trying to create a hero, refresh your memory about their physical features. Listening to a modern hero's dialogue can add depth to your understanding. The greater its quantity, the higher the likelihood of your success.

Travel abroad.

Do you desire to visit the Great Wall of China? The Pyramids? More is achievable in lucid dreaming. Regarding heroes, acquire thorough knowledge of your desired dream destination. Visual and written content of the place helps connect your mental dots to materialize its ambiance.

Arriving there is simpler (and more affordable) than in reality. See Chapter 5 for an effective spinning method. Moving your body in a dream restarts your brain activity for vivid dreaming. Spinning will get you to your intended destination.

Time Travel

Consider revisiting a beloved memory, such as a childhood Christmas. Lucid dreaming allows for more than just personal time travel.

In order to project your ideal self into an obsolete reality, you need to have extensive knowledge of the era including the events, clothing, language, customs, buildings, and social norms. Time travel is demanding and advanced; it is a complex activity to experience. This adventure is best suited for history buffs. Preparation time can lead to success. View images from the desired time period before sleeping to aid in dream preparation.

Live your dreams by practicing.

Your aspirations are high, but you have yet to achieve them. Perhaps you aim to win an Oscar or deliver a victory address on the night of a major election. Perhaps you desire to acquire Flamenco dance skills or perform on stage as a singer.

You can try out life goals and dreams by lucid dreaming, as it is a free of cost activity. Readers, if you have experience with visualization, you're likely interested in lucid dreaming. Lucid dreaming is similar to visualization, but in this case, you control the action as if it were happening in real life. Although visualization can be similar, the employed consciousness differs. Lucid dreaming is more profound than waking consciousness.

Lucid dreaming is closely related to your subconscious work. Lucid dreaming allows dynamic contact with your subconscious. In lucid dreams, you participate in tasks related to your waking life. The visualization is a temporary and illusory reality that appears immediately.

Learn a Skill

Lucid dreaming surpasses visualization in consciousness. To prepare, research the skill you want to learn.

Perhaps you've always been interested in embroidery or carpentry but never acquired the skills. Start learning in the lucid dream space. If you can picture yourself performing a task, you can ultimately perform that task, according to the theory of visualization. Lucid dreaming intensifies that effect.

I want to learn how to play the flute. Listen to the experts and concentrate on the flute's sound. Imagine yourself performing the task, mirroring the hand gestures and breathing techniques. Be aware of the mouth shape needed to blow air through the instrument.

Sound is amplified in lucid dreams. Music has a tangible presence. As you dream, learn a new skill and apply it in the real world. If you can dream it lucidly, you can achieve it.

Talk to Animals

Landlords and Homeowners Associations' strict regulations prevent pet ownership for some. Your lucid dreams offer the freedom to choose your own characters without any limitations or restrictions.

Your dream creatures can range from a cute kitten to a tiny Chihuahua to a powerful Siberian tiger (be cautious with the latter).

Use familiar domestic animals for this purpose. You're familiar with their actions and can anticipate them. Begin with a pet, perhaps a childhood companion or a cherished pet who has passed away. What would your animal companion tell you? How would you address your animal?

Perhaps you simply desire a calm moment to snuggle with a beloved pet who has passed away and whom you miss dearly. Perhaps you desire to engage with untamed birds or coyotes. Focus on the characteristics of your desired animal(s) and intend to visit them in your lucid dreams.

Solve Problems

Lucid dreaming can help solve real-life problems. Here, it is crucial to ask appropriate questions.

If you're feeling unhappy or stuck in a job or relationship, the dream space is where you can uncover the root cause.

Manifest a dream version of yourself to communicate with. We frequently ignore difficult thoughts as we continue living. The problem persists, and incurs costs. It grows in our minds' darkness, transforming into negative thoughts and subsequent behaviors, worsening the situation.

Being truthful about your desires and necessities is key to identifying the underlying issue. The non-judgmental dreamscape is sometimes the sole location for that type of work. No one can pass judgment here. We are incapable of self-judgment. We seek information to inspire positive action.

Get Intimate

Singles must take sex and COVID19 seriously. Other communicable illnesses should also be considered as potential encounters in the real world, not only COVID19. The space of lucid dreams is a safe outlet for sexual exploration.

You may be unsure about your sexual orientation. Is there a better place to question than a lucid dream? As the one in control, you can design your partner down to the smallest details.

You drive the action as you're in control. Your dream partner won't just appear out of nowhere. You are responsible for this task. Enter with confidence, acknowledging yourself as the architect and director. Have sex without worries of getting an STD or pregnant. Keep in mind that lucid dreams are solely for enjoyment.

Wander at Will

Women will be particularly drawn to this aspect of lucid dreaming. Women often fear lurking predators when going to desired locations. Women may enjoy a nocturnal view in their vivid dreams.

Picture yourself freely wandering in the moonlit night, relishing in the sounds without worry. The clearer your pre-sleep visualization, the larger your territory. You'll uncover a new world while journeying forward. Non-existence in reality enhances its beauty, doesn't it? It's yours. You are free to explore the night without fear.

Eat!

Are food allergies restricting your cooking choices? Perhaps you refrain from some foods due to gluten or lactose sensitivity. Perhaps food consumption leads to weight gain without visual observation.

I've developed an allergy to shellfish, but I still love it. Lucid dreaming is the solution. In my lucid dreams, I indulge in all the crawfish etouffee and lobster with drawn butter I desire, despite the fact that it's the worst thing for a shellfish enthusiast.

Visualize beyond your preferred cuisine. Remember the flavor, aroma, appearance, and feel of the food in your mouth. Recall maximum details prior to entering lucid dreaming. Enjoy your meal without feeling guilty or getting hives!

I hope this chapter provides enough information for you to create your own lucid dream landscapes and activities. We'll now discuss spirit guides and their role in enhancing lucid dreaming.

The Definition Of Lucid Dreaming

What is a lucid dream? In simple terms, it's the dream you can control. Frederik Willem van Eden created this term. He employed this phrase in his 1913 publication A Study of Dreams, coinciding with Freud's The Interpretation of Dream release year. To begin this chapter, let me share some definitions from well-known authors of lucid dreaming books.

Joseph McMoneagle cited Stephen LaBerge, Ph.D. of Stanford University Sleep Research Center, who explained that lucid dreaming is the state of "being awake in your dreams," not to be confused with daydreaming, which is "dreaming when you are awake." Daydreaming is not sleeping. When we are awake in our dreams, we are conscious while we sleep. We have a sleeping part and an awake part. We acknowledge that it is a dream. This is why lucid dreaming is also known as conscious dreaming.

Lucid dreaming is being aware and able to control one's dreams, as defined by Rebecca Turner in her book, The Art of Lucid Dreaming: The Pursuit of Conscious Dream Control. Consciousness is necessary to manipulate dreams. Lucid dreaming and dream control have long been used interchangeably.

According to a scientific article by Front Psychology Journal, a lucid dream is a dream in which the dreamer is aware they are dreaming, as defined by experts Daniel Erlacher, Melanie Schadlich, Tadas Stumbrys, and Michael Schredl. This definition is from LaBerge's work, rephrased slightly.

Professor Berit Broogard D.M.Sc., Ph.D. defined lucid dreaming as an opportunity to utilize the undiscovered capabilities of the brain.

Lucid dreaming is a dream that is both clear and controllable. What makes lucid dreaming special if it is the case? Experts did not prioritize lucid dreaming over ordinary dreaming. Lucid dreaming is believed to lack both function and meaning, unlike ordinary dreaming. Broogard said it's an opportunity to experiment. Only a performance. Don't worry about my low-priced lure. Lucid dreaming helps unleash extraordinary abilities in unused parts of your brain without requiring interpretation, as stated by Broogard. Boogard said you can be a superman in your dream, while I believe that being human is already super, as these extraordinary abilities are hidden in our subconscious mind. Lucid dreaming enables the conscious recognition of the subconscious mind's capabilities.

www.ingramcontent.com/pod-product-compliance
Lightning Source LLC
Chambersburg PA
CBHW050252120526
44590CB00016B/2320